Benja...

Ameri...

Colleen Adams

Rosen Classroom Books and Materials
New York

Published in 2002 by The Rosen Publishing Group, Inc.
29 East 21st Street, New York, NY 10010

Copyright © 2002 by The Rosen Publishing Group, Inc.

Book Design: Ron A. Churley

Photo Credits: Cover, p. 1 © Topham/The Image Works; pp. 5, 10, 22 © PhotoWorld/FPG International; pp. 6, 9, 13, 15, 17, 21 © Corbis-Bettmann; pp. 18–19 © Archive Photo.

ISBN: 0-8239-8237-8
6-pack ISBN: 0-8239-8640-3

Manufactured in the United States of America

Contents

Young Ben

Benjamin Franklin was born in Boston, Massachusetts, on January 17, 1706. At that time, Massachusetts was an English **colony**. Ben was the fifteenth of seventeen children.

Ben grew up working in his father's candle and soap shop. When he was ten years old, he finished school. When he was twelve, he was expected to learn a trade. Ben's father wanted him to work with his older brother, James, in the printing business.

As a young boy, Ben worked at his father's candle and soap shop in Boston.

Learning a Trade

Ben liked the printing business. He spent much of his free time writing short stories. He also wrote newspaper articles for his brother James's newspaper, the *New-England Courant.*

Ben did not like working as an **apprentice** in his brother's print shop. He worked long hours, but was paid very little. At the age of seventeen, Ben moved to Philadelphia, Pennsylvania, to find a job he would enjoy.

While he was working for the *New-England Courant,* Ben wrote stories using the name "Mrs. Silence Dogood."

Life in Philadelphia

At that time, Philadelphia was the largest city in the English colonies. Ben soon found a job as a printer and made new friends.

In 1728, Ben and a friend bought a print shop. In 1729, they began to publish a newspaper called the *Pennsylvania Gazette*. Ben wrote funny stories and articles for the newspaper. He married Deborah Read in 1730, and they began raising a family.

As a young man, Ben ran his own printing press and newspaper.

Poor Richard's Almanac

In 1732, Ben wrote a book called *Poor Richard's Almanac* (ALL-min-ack). An almanac is a type of book that has a calendar, maps, weather **forecasts**, and funny sayings.

People loved the book, and it was very successful. It sold over 10,000 copies a year. Ben wrote a new almanac each year for the next twenty-five years using the name Richard Saunders.

Poor Richard's Almanac was one of the best-selling books written during Ben Franklin's time.

Ben Studies Electricity

Ben had a scientific mind. In 1752, he performed a dangerous experiment to prove that lightning was really electricity. Ben made a kite with a metal wire at the top and tied a metal key to the kite string.

He and his son flew the kite in a lightning storm. The wire picked up an electric charge from the lightning. The electric charge moved down the kite to the metal key, proving that Ben's idea was right.

Ben became famous in the United States and Europe for making an important discovery about electricity.

A Famous Inventor

Ben invented many items that people still use today. In 1744, he invented a stove made of cast iron that looked like an open fireplace. This was called the Franklin stove. It was popular because it used very little wood but gave off a lot of heat.

Ben also invented **bifocals**. These glasses had one kind of lens on the top for seeing far away and a different kind of lens on the bottom for seeing close-up.

Ben liked to invent things, like bifocals, that would be useful to other people.

I therefore had former
Spectacles which I say
as in traveling I sometimes
then wanted to regard the
Finding this Change troublesome
always sufficiently ready. I ha
Glasses cut, and half of each he
sociated in the same circle, thus

Changes for the Community

Ben was always thinking of new ways to improve his community. In 1753, he was put in charge of the post offices for all the colonies. To make mail get places faster, Ben hired more mail carriers. He had some people work during the day and others work at night. Ben also started the first fire department, police force, and public library.

During Ben Franklin's time, mail carriers rode on horseback to deliver the mail.

Working for Change

In 1757, Ben went to England to try to solve disagreements between the colonies and England. Many colonists believed that England was asking them to pay an unfair amount of taxes.

For many years, Ben traveled back and forth between the countries to find an answer to the problem, but he was unsuccessful. Ben returned to America in 1775, shortly after the start of the **Revolutionary War**.

The colonists chose to fight for their freedom when their disagreements with England could not be worked out.

Shaping a New Nation

Ben was appointed to **Congress** and was asked to help write the **Declaration of Independence** in 1776. With these famous words, the colonists stated their freedom. They did not want to answer to England anymore. Ben helped **represent** the colonists in forming their own laws for the government of the new country, the United States of America.

Ben Franklin, Roger Sherman, John Adams, and Robert Livingston helped Thomas Jefferson write the Declaration of Independence.

Ben's Gifts

In 1776, Ben went to France to ask the French for help in the war against England. The French agreed. After the United States won the war, 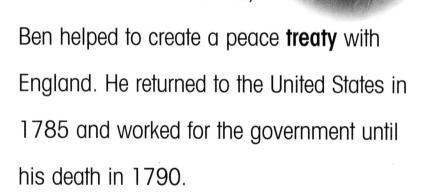 Ben helped to create a peace **treaty** with England. He returned to the United States in 1785 and worked for the government until his death in 1790.

Ben's work still affects us. He was an important inventor, leader, and **peacemaker** in the history of the United States.

Glossary

apprentice   Someone who learns a trade by working with a skilled worker.

bifocals   Glasses with a section for helping a person see things that are far away and a section for seeing things that are close-up.

colony   Land that has been settled by people who live in one country but are ruled by another.

Congress   A branch of the United States government that makes laws for the whole country.

Declaration of Independence   A public statement written by Congress on July 4, 1776, in which the thirteen colonies announced their freedom from England.

forecast   What it is thought the weather will be like at a future time.

peacemaker   A person who helps people find answers to their disagreements.

represent   To speak or act in place of someone else.

Revolutionary War   The war the English colonies fought to win freedom from England.

treaty   A written agreement between two nations.

23

Index